DEDICATION

To my four sons David, Michael, Paul, and John and five grandchildren Danny, Aiden, Sean, Katelyn, and Johnny, from whom I learned my greatest lessons in life so far.

I am also grateful to all my clients and friends, old and new, who have given me so much support.

You are Psychic

You are Psychic

Patricia Keegan

To order additional copies of this book, contact:
Xlibris Corporation
0-800-644-6988
www.Xlibrispublishing.co.uk
Orders@Xlibrispublishing.co.uk
303818

CONTENTS

FOREWORD

*I*n 2007, my son asked me to take care of my two small grandchildren for a week, while he and his wife sorted out their lives. I didn't see or hear from them for another three years. This was an unexpected event that suddenly changed my life.

I had spent a large portion of my life working at spiritual healing, psychic and spiritual readings, and clairvoyant demonstrations in England, America, and Spain. Lots of people, in the process, were curious as to how I was able to give so much information about them without having met them before.

After numerous questions-and-answer sessions and lots of training at the Arthur Findlay College in Stansted, I felt an urge to teach other people how to use their psychic abilities.

I held many psychic workshops, developing circles and groups, on this subject. While doing so, it struck me how very sincere people were with their wish, to not only exercise their psychic muscles, but also fulfill their inner spirituality. People were becoming more appreciative of what they had. I too was learning rapidly from my students.

After the children arrived, I took on a whole new way of life.

Every second was devoted to looking after my charges. I was forced to stand back from my work for a while. A whole new way of learning was taking place! Without the knowledge I had gained, I don't know if I could have coped.

As the children got older and less demanding, I occasionally got a glimpse of this workbook in my head.

However, it was a few years later that I was able to spend time putting it into print.

I hope people will benefit from this handy little book and use it both as a reference and as a learning tool. The exercises are simple yet effective. The chapters are an insight into what you can achieve. Subjects can be very diverse. By keeping it simple, you have the opportunity to learn from the basic information I have given you. This is how I started. I became greedy for information as I suspect you will too. By whetting your appetite, you can continue to learn as much as you want about each subject in due course.

Take your time with your development and practice as much as you can but always at your own pace.

I hope that all of you who are led to my book find it as exciting to learn from as I have found writing it.

So would you like to develop your sixth sense?

If so, I will take you on a journey of mysticism and joy and lead you to experience a whole new way of life because 'You Are Psychic!'

CHAPTER 1

Develop Your Talent

Thousands of ordinary people, just like you, are discovering how to become psychic consultants just by cultivating their natural abilities!

In this book, I will show you how to develop your talent to a professional level. You can then use it to help many people, if you so desire. Have faith; you can do it.

Even if you do not show any obvious signs, it is a fact that we all possess some psychic aptitude. This can be enhanced with patience and the right training. With over twenty years' experience, I can show you the pitfalls and benefits of fulfilling your dreams. Being able to help other people realise their inner strength through my work is one of the most rewarding jobs I have ever had. With the right motives, you can do it too.

With the exercises I show you and your own dedication, you could well be on your way to a new and satisfying career. There is nothing to stop you but yourself.

Lots of people find that when they start this journey, their understanding of life becomes clearer. The true purpose of life is to be happy. Understanding how is the sole key.

I am frequently asked if one has to be born with a special gift to be psychic. When I answer that everyone is psychic, they are often amazed.

It is an ability that we are all capable of developing.

In truth, it is a natural phenomenon that has been practiced from the beginning of time.

All children are psychic, and I was no exception.

When I was a child, I would instinctively know when things were going to happen. I also had prophetic dreams. I once dreamt that I found some sixpenny coins, covered by linoleum, in our home. Next day Mum decided to spring-clean the dining room. All the furniture was taken out and the floor covering removed. Imagine our excitement when we lifted the flooring and discovered lots of sixpences underneath—just as in my dream.

In those days we were quite poor. It was a lovely surprise for us all.

Unfortunately, it has been the custom, probably through fear, to ridicule children's second sight as imagination. This leads to a suppression of the gift, which is sometimes lost forever. I believe, if we listen to our children with understanding, their abilities would develop naturally as they grow. It's not hard to listen to a child and just go along with what they say. For instance, when my eldest son was about four years old, he would describe people he was seeing. I would listen to him reassuring him that it was all fine and nothing would hurt him. Some people are not able to do this, but rather, through their own ignorance, (which leads to fear) tell the child that there is nothing there. Instilling fear within the child is to try and suppress his instincts.

Lots of people have been led to believe that to use our inner sense is a bad thing. The first Witchcraft Act came into force in 1541, during King Henry V111's reign, but long before that, people were being burnt at the stake for simply using herbs as medicines. No wonder, people were frightened to develop their own ability.

So now is the time to regain what has been buried for so long. We have stepped into an enlightened age, and there are many opportunities around if you but look. When the pupil is ready, the teacher will appear. This is your chance to make your mark in the world and become a happier person in the process.

Sometimes, you will feel you have become stuck with your learning and are not progressing. Never worry about this. You are resting your faculty whilst getting ready for the next important phase. Your stomach cannot digest your breakfast, dinner, and tea all in one go. Small pieces at regular intervals make much more sense. Keep up with your meditation and stay relaxed at these times.

It may be that a development group would be helpful to you. Remember, when the pupil is ready the teacher will appear. Also, you may want to keep a journal. It will prove invaluable later on. Events may follow a pattern and only become clear when you follow signs. When you look back, you will see how much you have learned at that time.

Before embarking on this workshop manual, you should satisfy yourself that you are not suffering from any form of mental or emotional problems. As with any course of study, you will be using your thoughts as much as anything else, and therefore, it could exacerbate your problem. It would be much wiser to wait until any such illnesses are cured.

However, meditation is safe and will help in any given situation.

Work through the exercises at a sensible pace. As with exercising any muscle, too much too soon could ruin everything. You will get no further ahead, and it could impede your progress. So make time for the ordinary mundane things in your life. Slow your pace, and above all, enjoy your experiences.

CHAPTER 2

Meditation

The first step to any self-development is meditation. The more one meditates the more enlightened one becomes.

It relaxes the mind and opens up the doorway to many paths of understanding. It helps one become focused and stay that way. Your concentration span will become more efficient the more you practice. It is important to meditate regularly. At first, you can start with five minutes a day and gradually work your way up to about twenty minutes. Over the years, you may find that you want to double this but initially twenty minutes is probably enough. If you can do meditation at the same time each day, then it is good discipline. If this is impossible, don't worry as long as you keep up the practice.

As one meditates, one becomes full of cosmic energy. This is the same energy that renews us while we sleep. In meditation, however, it is more profound. This energy is essential for us to carry out our normal mundane tasks. We sometimes need some extra energy.

A good example of this is when we are exercising our psychic muscles.

You may notice irritability in your nature. This is because you are using the nervous system in development. Meditation and rest from psychic activity will soon remedy this.

Cosmic energy exists everywhere, particularly in nature.

Have you ever noticed how clear your mind seems after a solitary walk down a country lane?

Sit by a stream and feel the natural energy of the water cleanse you. This noticeable change brings peace and stillness that was, perhaps, missing before. A meditative walk through a forest of pine trees brings this energy, which is essential for us to carry out normal everyday tasks. It is also a still mind which brings peace. Sleep is unconscious meditation. When we meditate consciously, we receive the same energy in abundance.

So what is meditation?

It is the stilling of the mind to open up to universal energy in order to transcend the mind. When one starts to practice meditation on a regular basis, one embarks on a journey of self-discovery and knowledge that is available to all who seek. All our questions will be answered, sometimes during the meditation itself, or at a time and in a way unexpected by us. Take notice of subtle signs.

For instance, I once asked if it was good for me to do a certain thing. The answer came when I was driving behind a lorry, later on in the day.

Written in huge letters across the back of the lorry was:.

'It's good for you!'

Another time, I was asking myself what to do about a problem that I had. Later, when I was flicking through a magazine, the answer seemed to jump out at me whilst reading a poem. You may also find that the answer comes when someone makes a random comment, which is pertaining to your question. Or a thought may just pop into your head quite suddenly. Take notice of the signs.

You have the answers to all your questions inside of you. Trust and belief will strengthen your psychic ability.

So how do we do meditation?

You may find it easier to do a guided meditation at first. Here is a simple one you may like to record. Or you may find one that suits you at a store.

Exercise

Set aside a time when you will not be disturbed or distracted. Turn off the telephone.

Then seat yourself in a comfortable position—my personal preference is an upright chair, but as long as you are comfortable, that's all that matters.)

Relax. Close your eyes.

Now take three slow diaphragmatic breaths—that is, when you breathe in push your stomach out, and when you breathe out, let your stomach relax. It feels strange at first, but with practice it becomes natural. It is the correct way to breathe.

Now, let your breath return to normal. Relax. Try to still your mind and listen to your breath. Any unwanted thoughts can be gently pushed to one side. Come back to the breath and relax. Be patient when thoughts return. It happens to us all. Keep moving them to one side and return to observe your breath. Relax. Don't get annoyed; otherwise you will lose the state you have already reached. Just stay calm. You may see swirling colours or flashes of light while you are in this state. Observe them, and stay relaxed. At this point, you may feel a pulling or itching sensation in the region of your third eye, the space between the eyebrows, as it becomes activated. This is the opening of the doorway that leads to self-knowledge and beyond. We are receiving abundant cosmic energy. This is the state we want to achieve. Observe what happens in this time. Stay here for as long as you want, be it a few minutes or even longer. When it is time to return, come back to your breath. Take your time and wake up gradually. Wriggle your hands and feet, and when you are ready, open your eyes.

Now write an account of the whole experience. Do not forget to add the date.

Sit in a comfortable position.

Take three diaphragmatic breaths and then let your breath return to normal.

Imagine yourself walking along a tree-lined country lane. On either side of you, there are flowers in the hedgerows. You can smell their fragrance as you pass by. As you continue down this lane, you hear the trickling of a stream. You stop to rest by the stream and feel yourself receiving abundant cosmic energy from the plants and trees. You feel very safe and very relaxed here; run your hand in the water and just feel it renewing your soul. All worries and cares are gone. You hear the birds singing and look up to see a beautiful white swan that comes to rest beside you; he is very approachable and is offering to take you on a journey. You feel happy to accept his offer. He takes you soaring across the sky until he rests on a grassy bank. From your vantage point, you can see below the trees, the stream, and the country lane. You rest in this place feeling safe, secure, and very comfortable until it is time to return.

Here time a five minute break to relax

Now, you sense that your beautiful bird has returned. You climb upon his soft back and snuggle down. You feel very safe. He takes you back to the stream, and you begin your journey home along the country lane. You see the flowers on either side of the lane exactly as they were before. Now you find, you are back in your seat. You feel refreshed and ready to return to your day.

Write down your experience and date it.

I must tell you of my very first experience of meditation. I had just started to relax. Deeper and deeper I went. Suddenly, there was a loud cracking noise across the ceiling and down the walls. I instinctively ducked and opened my eyes. I thought the ceiling had caved in, but to my surprise, everything was as it had been with no sign of damage anywhere. I took this as a sign from heaven that I was at last on my true path. I had many opportunities in the past for developing my abilities, but I had declined every time. For instance, when I was a young woman, I had a particularly bad time as I was going through a divorce. I felt very lonely, so when I met up with an old friend from schooldays, I was glad of the company. I found out many things from my old friend. One evening when she came to visit me, we spent the day together, and when we put the children to bed, she suggested we play the Ouija board. She wrote out the letters of the alphabets and the words 'yes' and 'no'. She placed them in a circle on a small table and put a tumbler in the middle. The glass started moving immediately, and I was excited. My excitement soon vanished, however, when the force proved itself malevolent by the language it was spelling out. When my friend told it to stop, it began to spin round the table at an alarming pace. She told it to behave, but it shot off the table and landed across the other side of the room. My friend then threw the glass outside smashing it into a thousand pieces. Then she said, 'that's gone,' and she went home, leaving me alone to deal with my own emotions.

I went to bed and fell asleep immediately, but at one o' clock in the morning, I felt my arms and legs being stretched out in the shape of a cross. I looked around the room expecting to see someone there. I sensed a male spirit in the room with me. As he came close, I shuddered. I felt so afraid. I had no training and did not know what to do. I prayed to God to keep me safe. Each time he came closer, I trembled as I felt him trying to penetrate my aura. I clutched the tiny cross around my neck saying I believe in God, over and over again, until he finally left. The next day, a neighbour said she knew a lady that she thought could help me. I went to see her, and she invited me to go along to church with her. I agreed, but when my neighbour told me she would be taking me to a spiritualist church, I thought to myself, *I'm trying to get rid of spirits not attract more.* So I did not go.

If I had gone, it would have probably saved me a lot of heartache later on. It's not the events that happen in your life, but your ability to cope with them. I have learned so much since those early days.

Like attracts like, and my friend had chosen to get involved with black magic. I knew nothing of this at that time. So the lost spirit was trying to find a like-minded soul. My fear gave him power. Had it not been for my strong belief in God, the Protector, I would not have had the strength to ward him off. I tell you this story in the hope that you may learn from it. If its excitement and games you want, there is always someone to comply.

Developing with love in your heart, for the benefit of other people as well as yourself will ensure you have a safe and happy journey.

A few years later, my friend Christine's father died, and she asked me to go to a spiritualist church with her. Had she been going on her own, I definitely would have gone to support her. As it was, there was a crowd going, so I declined her offer.

Both times, I was being pointed in the right direction; both times, I refused to go. It was much later that I discovered what this pathway had to offer me.

Meditation is the key to all knowledge. Whatever skills you are trying to develop will be greatly enhanced with the help of your 'in-tuition'—teaching from within. Strive to be the best you can.

Everyone has different experiences. That's what makes us unique. Do not model yourself on anyone else, however great you may think they are. You have the potential to become even better.

I always include meditation in my teaching as the first step in development. The reason for this is that we develop our own persona at the same time.

CHAPTER 3

Affirmations

What is an affirmation?

An affirmation is a thought that reaffirms itself in one's subconscious mind and then works itself out in our everyday lives.

It is very important, when embarking on any new project, that one understands fully the importance of what one says or thinks and how it affects one's progress.

For example, if one is forever thinking that they cannot achieve something, guess what? This thought settles in the subconscious mind and gradually works itself out in the conscious mind to become an actuality.

This is a fact that successful people know. People in marketing use this strategy to get results in business. It's something we can all do. We must believe in our own abilities. It's one of the most powerful tools we have. Confidence grows when you regularly affirm that nothing is beyond you.

A friend of mine had lost her confidence after going through a particularly harrowing divorce. She was continually finding fault with herself and everyone around her. Everything in her life, it seemed, was going wrong; she was feeling more and more depressed as time went on. She verbally used the 'affirmation' that everything in her life always went wrong. I tried to explain how thought patterns worked, but as with so many, she was not ready to listen. This has to come to you of your own accord.

As time went by, she found she missed having someone to share her life with but had very low self-esteem—finding fault with everything she did.

I had told her how powerful her thoughts were and how she could use them to her advantage. However, she was still not ready to listen then and chose to continue in her usual way.

The time came, however, when she became desperate for some change.

She asked me again, 'How can you be sure your theory will work for me?'

I told her my story, how I had used my thoughts to heal my life at a time when I was so desperately unhappy that life didn't seem worth living.

My body was a mirror of what I was going through inside. I was unable to walk properly and was undergoing physiotherapy. The excruciating pain in my back and the pains in my joints reflected my life perfectly. It was crumbling around me, and I was too.

One morning, I woke up from my bed, and I could not see properly. It was as though someone had pulled a curtain across my face, and I was just able to peep out through a hole in it. The rest was completely black—there is none so blind as those who do not wish to see. I did not want to experience any more pain, emotionally or physically. I was choosing to let my circumstances rule my life. I did not know that I had the power to control my own situation. We cannot change what is happening around us, but we can change the way in which we let it affect us. It was at this time that the words of 'Go Forward' came to me in a poem.

Go Forward
If this world is not what you want it to be
Create the one you do
Shun corruption and violence
The peace is inside of you

Look and you will find it
Search and you will see
That whatever goes on around you,
You have the option to flee

Not from the world, that you cannot escape
But from the torment it carries instead.
Don't lose your trust, in God's love have faith, and release the
dead from your head.

Go forward with a clear conscience,
Let go of the damaging past.
Trust and faith are all you need,
You can now let it go at last.

Yesterday's fears are yesterday's sorrows,
Leave them where they belong
Yesterday *is* Yesterday
Go forward now, be strong.
Face your fears and watch them run
You have always done so before.
Don't start to decline go forward you're fine.
You know that this is God's law!

The turning point came in my life when I joined the spiritualist church in Bury St. Edmunds where I lived. I had gone there specifically to learn about spiritual healing.

After the service, I met a couple, and we became absorbed in conversation. We became firm friends after that, and as time progressed, we sat in a development group at my house for many years together. I received a lot of healing from that group and developed my talent as a medium and as a healer. It was during this time that my friends gave me a book called, *'Thought Forces'* by Prentice Mulford. It was this book that started me off on an enlightening journey that has made me into the woman I am today. I read it every day and practiced the theory that thoughts are living things! By your thoughts so shall you be. It took a long time and didn't happen immediately. Old habits are difficult but not impossible to remove. But gradually over the years, I have used my thoughts to shape my life.

It was Christmas, and I saw a mirror for sale. It was in the shape of a joker. It reminded me of my son. It was exactly the sort of thing he appreciated. It reminded me of when he was in the school play as a little boy. He played a brilliant part as a joker and stole the show.

He seemed to have lost his spark lately and needed a boost. He was slipping into an unhealthy depression and was very critical of himself. I was worried.

'It's an affirmation mirror!' I announced. He laughed. I could see he appreciated it!

'Every morning when you get up, look in the mirror and tell yourself,

'I love you. You look marvellous.'

He laughed. 'People will think I am crazy,' he said.

'I am full of confidence.' 'I have all that I need.'

Still laughing, he looked in the mirror and said, 'Hello handsome,' then roared with laughter. We both had tears in our eyes with laughter when I left him.

'Try it religiously for a week,' I said, 'Every time you catch yourself in the mirror.'

He did it more than a week and laughed when I next saw him. 'I think I am getting used to this,' he said. 'I am becoming obsessed.'

'Well, you look happier anyway,' I said. The results were amazing. He made positive steps towards a happier life. Changing the things he didn't like. When he met the love of his life, he said he felt his life was complete!

When you accept yourself exactly the way you are, you will accept other people as they are too. This makes life run so much more smoothly as you will not get stressed about other people's habits. Obviously, as lessons in one's life become difficult, it's easy to forget. But if you start your affirmations again, over time, life gets better.

Whatever one affirms, it must be right for that person. One should choose one's words carefully. Sometimes, we think we know what we need but don't think about the consequences of it. Our higher selves know exactly what is good for us. Sometimes, we will get what we need rather than what we want.

Now he had accepted the first step, I explained to him how appreciation worked hand in hand with affirmations. When you show the universe the things you appreciate in life, it works to add more of these things to your life.

Exercise

Have a pencil and some paper ready. Sit in a comfortable position, close your eyes, and take three diaphragmatic breaths as described earlier. Start to think of all the good things you have in your life. Don't forget the obvious: people, food, shelter, love, etc. Spend at least five minutes just appreciating and thanking the Universe for these things. Say them loudly, or say them in your mind, but keep repeating them. When you have done this, pick up your paper and write them down. Do this every time you think of it. See how long your list becomes as you get used to doing this exercise. It may be difficult at first. If I were to ask you, however, to make a list of everything you want, I am sure it would be easier. You can use the wish list later in the same way. But show the world what you appreciate first!

The point is, we are always looking for someone else or something to make us happy. The only way we can be truly happy is by loving ourselves exactly as we are.

With an understanding of affirmations, one can use them to achieve anything.

We must remember, however, that we can also use our thoughts in a negative way. If one is always complaining about the things they have in their lives, affirmations will work to remove these things. So be careful about what you say, and don't complain about the things that you really could not do without. Don't forget, the subconscious mind takes everything literally.

Understanding how one's thoughts work and whether what we verbalise works for or against us is a useful tool. The study of affirmations will help you transform your health, your wealth, and happiness from that which you already have to that which you truly need. Listen carefully to how others speak, and watch what they create.

Realising that we do not have to accept what is thrust upon us helps one to change things for the better and gives us the scope we need to achieve any goals we want.

> Our mind is a complex and mystical thing. Mystical because it is so little understood. Being aware of how it works has to be considered. There are three parts to our brain, that is the unconscious, the subconscious, and the conscious mind. The unconscious mind is a bank of memories and feelings that one holds on to. Usually, these thoughts are too painful to remember and yet according to Freud, these thoughts still continue to affect our experience of life.

> The subconscious makes up ninety per cent of the total mind. It makes sense that one should try and put in as many positive thoughts in the subconscious as we can so we may deal with this accumulation of ideas.

> What we imprint on this part of the brain will eventually work itself out in the conscious mind.

> One's conscious mind holds things we are totally aware of in our ordinary life. Part of this includes memory; from this space we can retrieve information from our subconscious mind at any given time. Freud called this the preconscious mind. If you want to learn more about this you take a course on psychology.

However, this is the basis of how affirmations work. But it is not enough to simply do affirmations. It is the combination of actually taking steps to achieve your goals and confirming that you will achieve them.

When I was a child, my parents constantly impressed upon me that I was second best to the next person. I was told I was a nuisance and had spoiled my mother's life. I do not blame her for this; however, I am just stating a fact that affected my personality early on in life. We are all affected in some way by what was affirmed in our early life.

These false beliefs are like an indelible mark on the brain and are not easily removed. However, it is possible to turn things around and just take the positive from our experiences by creating new beliefs.

Consequently, I grew up with a huge chip on my shoulder. It affected the way I thought of myself. I always put other people before myself and my own needs. Never expecting anything better, I never got it because according to my conditioning I did not deserve it.

I know that lots of other people have also been influenced by what they experienced when they were children.

I don't think people set out to be cruel; they are unaware of how powerful their words are and the impact they have.

I found it very helpful to work psychologically on myself with the aid of self-help books. I Understood that I had a powerful ability to be able to change my thoughts and turn my life around which gave me a goal in life.

Learning to become aware of one's power can have a massive impact.

Incorporate positive thoughts into your development, and you will achieve your goals. Believe in yourself. If you do not, no one else will either!

If you use affirmations like, 'I am a wonderful psychic.' regularly while you are training, you will boost your confidence and your progress.

Here is a checklist of how to do affirmations.

1. Be positive in everything you say. Never undermine yourself in any way, even as a joke. Your subconscious mind has no sense of humour and will work things out according to what you say. If, for example, you break a cup, don't say, 'I am always breaking things'. The subconscious picks up the words 'always' and 'breaking' and works them out accordingly. So try not to even say the word breaking. It is a negative word. Rather, confirm that you are careful with things. Words create actions.

2. Make up a simple phrase for what you want to achieve, anything that is important to you. The simpler your phrase, the more you will remember it. Try not to use negative words in your phrase. For example, do not say, 'I will not forget.' But rather, say, 'I will remember'. Then you are not even putting the word forget into your mind. Be clear and precise about what you want. For example, if you are looking for a long-term relationship, remember to ask for the right person for you. I believe there is someone for everyone, but be sure to ask for the one you will be happy with.

3. Practice these affirmations as often as you think of them. Once or twice a day is not enough. Repeat over and over again. Sometimes, things work themselves out very quickly, while others may take longer. The art is to keep at it.

4. Act as if you have already received. This always conveys trust in the reality of the affirmations, enabling them to work efficiently.

5. Visualisation. Spend about five minutes at a time visualising yourself as you would like be. See yourself as healthy, happy, and contented, doing the work you would like to do. See yourself as the psychic consultant, if that's you want to be, helping lots of people achieve better lives for themselves. Hold on to these pictures as long as you can. If you can't see the pictures, and many cannot, it doesn't matter. Just know they are there. Practice as many times a day as you can.

6. Above all, be grateful for what you are receiving and for what you already have in your life. This, I have found, is especially effective for one's well-being. Look after, love, and cherish the people and things you enjoy, and show the Universe what you really want by declaring appreciation of them.

CHAPTER 4

Auras

What is an Aura?

Our aura is the energy field that surrounds the physical body in all directions. It is often from this that we get most of our information when working psychically. With practice, we can learn to see the aura and interpret what the colours mean. That means you can too. Everyone can develop this gift. Start off with simple exercises to sense the aura first.

Exercise

Stand behind your seated partner, and put your hands on their shoulders. Close your eyes and relax. Now, take your hands back, about a foot away. Still, with eyes closed and relaxing, try to sense the energy. You can put them back again and draw them away—feel the difference. You may feel a tingling sensation or warmth. This is unique to you, so make a mental note of how you perceive the energy. Your friend may also sense a pulling and withdrawing as you move your hands. This can be practiced with different people to see how their energies differ. Keep notes in your diary of all experiments.

These exercises are designed to help you detect the subtle energies around you, not just from individuals, but from the ether itself. Most people have walked in on an argument unexpectedly. Although the people concerned may try to cover it up, there is a strong atmosphere that one senses. This can be left behind even when the people concerned are gone.

You may walk into a place you never visited before and feel a sense of dread for no apparent reason if the area had been used for undesirable events. Trust your instincts. What you sensed are the energies left behind. Lots of people confuse this with spirit contact. It is not necessarily so. As you develop, you will differentiate between the two. Read the chapter on psychometry. Because you are psychic, it does not automatically follow that you are also a medium. Time will tell. A psychic receives information from the psyche of the person she is reading, for example, incarnate spirit. A medium receives information from outside the person, for example, discarnate spirit. But this is quite another and very diverse subject.

> We can train the eyes to see the aura with the use of eye exercises. Babies are born using the peripheral vision, that's why, sometimes we see them looking about and smiling at what we think is nothing. As we get older, we gradually stop using the peripheral vision and let the central vision take over. So to see the aura, we have to learn to use the peripheral vision all over again. But this can be done by anyone; we do not need any special tools.

> Let me explain a little about how the human eye works.

> There are two types of cells in the retina of the eye, the cone cells and the rod cells. Cone cells are bundled towards the centre of the retina. They are used by your central for everyday use. They register shades of light and colour.

> The rod cells are more numerous and are around the edge of the retina. These cells pick up what is on the edge of your field of view. This is the peripheral vision.

> The rod cells cannot differentiate between colours. They pick out contrast better than the cones. This explains the phenomenon that night vision is easier using your peripheral vision.

Exercise

Study the diagram below and concentrate on the black dot in the n...uuie. Bring your eyes slightly out of focus, and gaze steadily at the dot. You will notice you can still see the two circles, but don't look at them directly. You are now using the peripheral vision. Gradually, you will start to see the aura around each circle moving. At this stage do not try to analyse what you are seeing, just stay focused on the black dot. Next, they will look as if they are floating towards the middle to meet each other. This is the where you need to stay completely relaxed, and observe without shifting your eyes. What we are aiming at is for the two circles to come together to form one circle with a cross in the middle. This will take lots of practice, so persevere. Once you have achieved this, keep the picture for as long as you can. The more relaxed you are with this exercise, the easier it becomes.

Initially, you will only be able to hold it for a few seconds. The aim is to be able to hold it for about thirty minutes. However, you will find even a few minutes will be enormously beneficial.

We use our central vision most of the time. For seeing the aura, we need to employ our peripheral vision. This exercise will teach us to use both.

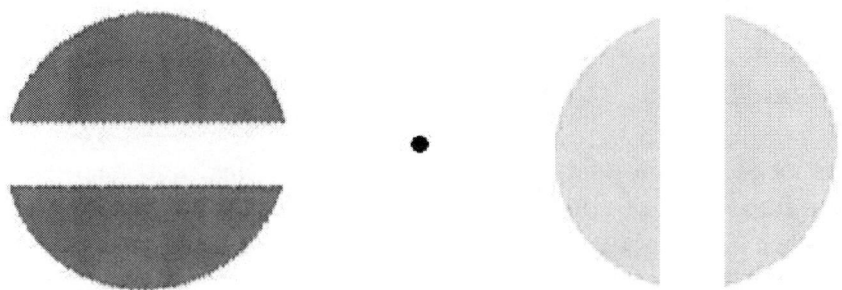

With your eyes out of focus, practice bringing the two circles together to form one with a cross in the middle. You need to persevere. Practicing a little and often is more successful than working for longer periods less often. You will surprise yourself, and it is well worth the effort. If you prefer, you could copy the diagram on to coloured sheets of paper and stick them on the wall somewhere.

So this is how one's eyes work. To see the aura, one must be in control of using both visions.

The key here, as with anything else, is to have patience and keep practicing.

This was how I saw the spirit of the little girl, who was watching me, while I lay in bed one morning. I saw her with my peripheral vision. This was an exciting first experience. I held this for as long as possible trying to keep a steady gaze. I knew that to hold the view I must not move my focus. I did it for quite a few minutes before my eyesight centralised and then I lost sight of her. I was disappointed that I lost my focus but also pleased I held it for so long.

It was like looking into the world of spirits. The two worlds are so closely interconnected that it is possible, with the right motives and patience, to bond with both.

Exercise

Work with a partner if you have one. If not, use a mirror where you can see yourself.

Stand or sit near a pale-coloured plain wall. Relax, and gaze steadily at the head area of your friend, or yourself if you are working alone, with your eyes slightly out of focus so that you are using your peripheral vision. It's like looking out of the corner of your eye. If you have done the exercise above, you may have already grasped the idea. The more you relax, the easier this becomes. What we are looking for is like a heat haze emanating from the head area. Hold this for as long as you can, and try to passively observe this without getting too excited otherwise it will be gone just as quickly. You may also notice it comes and goes as your eyes lose focus. As you become more experienced, you will begin to see colours in the haze. When you start to see this, you know you are truly progressing. I was thrilled when I first saw it. Then I started to get glimpses of colour around people when I wasn't even looking for them.

Here is a little about the energy field and how it works.

Our body is made up of atoms, protons, neutrons, and electrons that are so dense that they look and feel as if they are solid. Think of them as building blocks of matter. Surrounding this, we have our energy body, also called the etheric body, also made up of atoms. In the etheric body these atoms are not as concentrated, so they are not as solid. You can learn more about atoms, if you want, in basic anatomy—a fascinating subject, essential for those wishing to develop their healing abilities.

These energies around the physical body become finer and relate to the chakras. This is what is known as our auric field. As we interpenetrate with other people's energies, our aura isso penetrable, we should be aware of any negative energy we could be soaking up.

We have seven main chakras in our body. These are like vortexes that draw in energy and also emit them. In a healthy person they are continually spinning. Sometimes, they become sluggish or blocked and need to be re-energised. There are a variety of ways you balance your energy points yourself. It may also be done by a healer. But let's look at how the chakras work first.

Crown Chakra

Represented by the Colour Violet

This is located at the top of one's head and is associated with the colour violet.

This chakra is one's divine connection to the spiritual realms where wisdom and knowledge can be reached. You could develop this chakra through meditation as with all the other energy points.

The Third Eye

Represented by the Colour Indigo

This chakra is situated between the eyebrows. It is where our in-tuition—teaching from within—is stored. Through development of this chakra clairvoyance—clear seeing—can be obtained. From here you may open many doors to the inner world and beyond to transcend the psychical and gain access to other dimensions. To activate this chakra, meditate on the colour of indigo.

The Throat Chakra Represented by the Colour Blue

The third chakra is in the throat area and is responsible for speaking truths. This may become blocked if you do not express your feelings through your voice.

The Heart Chakra

Represented by the Colour Green

This one is in the region of your chest area, as expected, and becomes affected by relationships, sorrow, and a need to give and receive love.

The Solar Plexus Chakra

This is represented by the colour Yellow

This fifth chakra can be found in the space between the stomach and the breast. This is where all our emotional feelings are stored. Also, when we get a hunch, or a fear, or a gut feeling about something, it can be sensed here. It's been described as butterflies in one's tummy. This can also be experienced when getting ready to do healing or a reading. It's the energy building here that prepares you for the work at hand. Test these hunches and feelings, and make notes about them as you develop this faculty. It is the centre of one's power.

The Sacral Chakra

Represented by the Colour Orange

The sacral chakra is the next one down and this controls all stomach issues, relationships, and creativity.

The Root Chakra

Represented by the colour Red

One's sexuality, and security, job, money, and home are all based here.

These are the seven main chakras but there are many others throughout the body.

All chakras are connected by the meridian lines, through which essential life force, energy, or chi flows. You can think of these as tubes, like the veins in your body where the blood flows. Veins are necessary to take the blood to the heart. Meridian tubes take the energy from chakra to chakra to keep one in balance and harmony. By keeping these chakras clear and in good working order, one maintains a healthy body.

There are a number of ways you can do this one is by using a chakra meditation. This will help to keep the vortexes spinning to attract healthy energies to you. You can then keep them this way by regular use of this method.

Exercise

You may like to play some soothing music for this one. Sit in an upright chair, feet flat on the floor and hands resting in your lap. Take three deep diaphragmatic breaths. Breathe in slowly, and push your stomach out. Slowly breathe out, and let your stomach relax naturally. Start your exercise when you are feeling quite relaxed.

Imagine you have a beautiful flower on the crown of your head. Now, see the petals gently opening one at a time. When the flower is fully open, feel it drawing in the subtle energy from all around it.

Next, move down to your third eye chakra, and imagine the flower opening its petals and drawing in the universal energy.

Work down all seven chakras in the same way—opening the flowers and drawing-in the energy.

Visualise all seven vortexes bringing in this powerful life force to you. When you feel re—energised, you may begin to close the chakras down. Not too tightly, however, as you still want to allow a gentle flow in and out to maintain balance.

To close them down, start with your base chakra, and gently close the petals one at a time.

Move up to the sacral area and close the flower in the same way. Continue to close all the energy points in the same way, one at a time, petal by petal, until you finally reach the crown chakra. Now imagine you are drawing a protective white light all around the whole of your body and aura so that it looks like you are the whole body inside an eggshell.

Everything you have ever done shows up in the aura, sickness, illnesses, depression, and sadness. Sickness starts in the outer aura. It can be treated from here before it manifests in the physical body which takes about eighteen months. During this time, one's energy becomes exhausted. This is when the adrenalin gland activates through stress, which in turn causes a build-up of acid, leading to static electricity. Early detection of an imbalance can be treated before it sets. How beneficial is that! It makes me think that everyone should learn to read the aura. It is such a powerful tool.

CHAPTER 5

Healing

This was my first love. It is how I came into spiritualism. It was the springboard of my clairvoyance. I was told by a medium, when I was a young woman, that I had healing abilities as she could see a blue aura around my head. I was ignorant as to what she was talking about and didn't have the time or inclination to find out! It may have made my life easier if I had. I was, however, busy bringing up my four children.

Later on as one of my children grew up and became seriously sick, I remembered what I had been told. Wouldn't it be wonderful if I could cure him? We had already tried all the conventional methods. I was very troubled by his 'illness' but tried to carry on as normal.

At that time, I was working on an intricate design for a satin bedspread I was making. I went to the library to study some patterns to help me with it. My son was on my mind, and I found I could not concentrate and fell into a sort of dream. I walked across to the medical section and randomly pulled out a book called spiritual healing by Philippe Pillaw. I took it home and read it from cover to cover. When a friend came to visit me one day and saw it lying on the table, she asked me to practice it on her. I did, and she immediately found some relief in her frozen shoulder. From here, I went to try healing myself as I had been suffering terrible back pain. I had seen specialists and a physiotherapist but nothing seemed to help. After the third session of healing, over three consecutive weeks, it was gone. I telephoned The National Federation of Spiritual Healers in London to find out how to become a healer. We spoke at some length, and he put me in touch with someone who could train me. However, the person told me that I could also train at a Spiritualist Church. I decided to join the one in my home town of Bury St. Edmunds. The first time I went, the service had already started. I watched it, fascinated, through a window in the door. I listened to the medium make her address and the clairvoyance she did afterwards. I enjoyed it so much I vowed I would go back again. I joined the next service and after it had finished asked a girl if they did healing the church. She led me round to a little room at the rear of the building. There was soft music playing as I went in, and I sat attentively on a bench and watched the healers at work. While I dreamily watched one healer at work, I suddenly saw what I thought was smoke coming from his hands. Well, I didn't like the thought of that for a start! I immediately looked under his chair to see if there was an ashtray there. No sign of a cigarette anywhere, I am pleased to say. Then I looked around to see if there was a hot drink anywhere. Of course, there was not. I nudged the girl I was with. 'What is that smoke?' I said.

'What smoke?' she asked, screwing up her nose. I realised she could not see it. The next day, I phoned the president of the church, who told me it was the healing energy and that most people don't see it.

This episode was enough to convince me that I wanted to develop my healing gift here. I trained here under the healing group leader regularly for two years. I gave healing to everyone who asked, my son included. Some days, he had better than others. This was the springboard to my clairvoyance.

Using one's ability to heal others allows the healer to become healed in the process. I could not believe the dramatic change that occurred in my own health.

Spiritual healing is the use of universal energy. The energy is transferred from the higher powers through the medium and into the patient. Our planet is made up of energy in the trees and plants and power from the water and the sun. We are able to use this force from all the elements and conduit it to make use of it. The healer is used to transmit the power to the patient.

If you think of it, it's like electricity. You can't see it, but you know it's there by its strength. A transmitter is used to transfer electricity to where it is needed. Without a pylon, it is useless. It is the same with spiritual healing. It is being channelled through the medium. You need the medium to transfer the power.

Exercise

First of all, do a ten minute meditation and ask that you may be used as a healing channel. If you want, you can say a little prayer to that effect.

Try to recognise the healing power.

With a partner seated on a chair in front of you, place your hands very gently on their shoulders—always ask for permission first—or a few inches away from them.

Close your eyes, relax, and take three deep breaths.

Imagine that your whole body is being filled with Universal energy.

Allow the divine energy to flow out through your hands to the person. Notice how you feel when the energy starts to flow. You may feel warmth or tingling in your hands. You may feel a coldness across your head, or you may feel nothing at all. Either way, do not underestimate the strength of the healing power.

I have been asked why healing doesn't always work. I reply that it does. It may sound strange, but not everyone wants to be well. Some people hang on to their illnesses because they find it of some use to them. Think of the world as a huge school in which we learn the lessons of life. We choose our life according to the lessons we have to learn. Whether it is the lesson of pain or gratitude we choose our life to reflect this. Everyone has free will, however, and no one can be cured, unless they want to be. When one wants to be well, they will accept the healing given. Healing cannot be forced on anyone. One has the ability to accept or reject it. All healing works on some level, even if it is a person's karma to be ill or disabled. It can help one cope with the situation.

There are many healing courses you can take, one is The National federation of Spiritual Healers, or you can do as I did and join your local spiritualist church.

Courses usually run for about two years. While you are developing your gift, there are various other courses that may be helpful. I found first aid, basic anatomy, and counselling very useful. It is also a help to have contact numbers of any self-help groups.

CHAPTER 6

Psychometry

L ots of psychics use this method when they prepare to do a reading. You will probably surprise yourself when you first start practicing. It is a very good exercise and, if developed properly, can be very powerful and accurate.

It is the art of drawing information from an object about the person to whom it belongs. Some people see vivid pictures in their head, clairvoyantly, when they first start to tune in. Some experience pain or emotional feelings. Never pass these feelings off as your own. This is probably how the other person feels. So say everything that comes into your head. You may pick up the person's character or even what they were doing that very morning. The possibilities are endless.

Any object can be used for this as long as it belongs to that person. Any item will do for this exercise, a piece of jewellry perhaps, or a watch, or a key.

You can also practice with letters that come through the post. Hold the letter in your hand, close your eyes, and relax, take three deep breaths, and then concentrate on the letter.

Try to think about what's inside. Is it handwritten or typed, or is it black and white, or are there any other colours. Pick up as much information as you can from it. Don't despair if you get it all wrong. The important thing is that you are trying, and the more you practice the more adept you will become. You can also try this with a friend. Put something in an envelope, anything will do, a photograph, a library card, etc. Exchange your envelopes and start psyching in.

You can tell almost anything with psychometry. Archaeologists employ this practice when tuning into an ancient artefact they have found, to date the piece and get other impressions of what it was used for etc.

To do a reading using psychometry, one uses a personal object belonging only to that person. By consciously extracting information from it, we can begin to tell a little bit about that person's personality.

Exercise

Try to work with someone you don't know too much about. Ask them for an item of jewellry, a watch, or anything that is personal, and has belonged only to that person; otherwise, you may well find yourself tuning into the vibrations of the previous owner. The longer the person has owned it, the more energy it has absorbed from them.

Now, hold the object in your hands and relax. You should verbalise the first thought that comes into your head. Even if it doesn't make sense to you, it may to your recipient. How does the object feel, is it buzzing with energy or cool and calm. You are probably picking up the owners emotions. You must say everything you feel—otherwise you stop the flow of impressions you are getting.

Do you suddenly feel pain anywhere, lightheaded, or blissfully happy? Say so. Are you feeling nervous? You must say what impressions you are getting. Do not try to rationalise what you are sensing. Do you feel as if you can't say anything at all? You may be nervous, but don't necessarily put your silence down to that. Your friend may have an issue she needs to talk about but can't. So you see the importance of saying everything you get. He who never makes a mistake has never tried anything new. This is how one learns—through mistakes. So welcome your mistakes as lessons. Afterwards, ask your partner for feedback. You may be surprised to learn how much you got right.

Exercise

Try to work in a group if possible. The more people there are, the better it is. You may like to seat yourselves in a circle for this, but it is not essential. Put some paper, pencils, crayons and chalk, etc, in the middle so everyone can reach. Now you can draw a picture, write a poem, or even note just a couple of words. You may use colours or just lead pencil. Don't let anyone see it. Now fold up the pieces of paper and put them into a bag. Mix them up, and let everyone choose a piece of paper.

Now open it up, and try to figure out who this belongs to. See what impressions you get from the drawing or words. Let you imagination run riot. Write everything down. Even if it sounds silly, it doesn't matter, it is the actual tuning into the thing that's developing your ability. Each person then shows the paper to the group and reads out what they have written about it. Don't despair if nothing is right. You may be picking up feelings from something entirely different—the person sitting next to you, for example. If you keep practicing, you will learn to focus on the subject at hand.

Exercise

This is an exercise you can do when you are out and around with a friend. Go and have a look around an art gallery, or museum, or town hall, or old houses, in fact anywhere that you feel may hold some history. Both of you, put your hands on the walls and feel what you are sensing. Go to another part of the building, and see if feels different. Is it a light cheerful place, or is it heavy and oppressive? Write down what you feel and compare notes afterwards. Not at the time when you may influence each other. Now, try to find out as much information as you can about the place.

People use very interesting places to tune into, like restaurants, antique shops, workshops, and libraries. We can make the most of these venues to practice and also enjoy what is on offer at the same time. Make your learning fun. We learn so much more when we relax, and enjoy.

CHAPTER 7

Tarot

To do these exercises, it is useful to have a basic knowledge of the meanings of each card. This is a very useful tool when you first start out, although, it can evoke very strong feelings in some people. Some people say it is good to be given a pack of tarot cards and work with them. In my opinion, it is best to choose your own. Someone gave me a pack of tarot cards once. They showed me the basics of reading them, and I began to practice. The only trouble was, I did not like the feel of them. I did not particularly like the pictures, either. I persevered, however, because I had been given them and had read that was the best way to obtain them. So I read everything I could about the subject and listened to other people read their cards. It cost me a fortune just to see how other people used them. I did all this but to no avail. I was uncomfortable with the pack and had it in my mind that they were somehow evil. I remembered, when a child, hearing my mum say all cards were evil. My grandmother would never allow cards in the house because of this.

I tried, however, to get the better of the cards. Every time something went wrong, I blamed the cards. In the end, I threw them in the dustbin. I felt a wave of relief when I did this.

It wasn't until much later that I met an expert in tarot. I told her about my experience with the cards. She said that the old beliefs and the myths that surrounded the cards I had been using was blocking me from reading them. She also expressed that by reading and handling the cards I would help unfold my psychic ability.

This time, I chose my own cards. I looked at lots of packs, picking them up and handling them, until I felt drawn to one particular pack. The first thing my teacher told me to do was to throw away the instructions, which I did. Learn from the cards, she said. First of all, I handled them as much as possible. I treated them as I would something really precious. I slept with them under my pillow and began to have weird dreams. The dreams told me mysterious things, showed ancient Hebrew signs that I had no knowledge of. This prompted me to find out about the history of the Tarot.

I took them on every holiday that I went on, so they could be with me all the time. The energies of the cards and those of my own have mingled until I have become very much in tune with them.

I had begun on another pathway. It seemed strange, but even a friend of mine dreamed that she saw me using the tarot and invited me to work with her in her therapy clinic in London. I learned all I could about them and eventually overcame my fear of working with them.

I now have some lovely cards that I chose myself and completely resonate with them. I have used the same pack for about twenty years. This is a brilliant way to you use your gift of vision to help other people. I often find it works as a useful counselling tool. Some people will come to see you with a problem they need to solve. It's not until they see the cards laid out and the choices they have that they realise that they knew, within themselves, the answers to their own difficulties.

To work well with the tarot, you must resonate with them. Let them begin to put ideas in your head. They will be quite different from other people's ideas. Follow the clues they give you.

Exercise

You can do this in a group or on your own. Use a different card each time you do this exercise.

Have a pen and paper ready.

Choose one card from the pack. Stand it on a shelf so that you can see it clearly. Get yourself in a comfortable position and gaze into the picture. Look right into it as if you are climbing into it—a bit like the scene in Mary Poppins, where, they jump into Bert's pavement paintings. Sit for about ten minutes and then begin writing down your experiences. Then allow your imagination the freedom it needs to progress. Do this exercise every day with a different card. Have a pencil and your notebook ready. Stand the card in front of you on a shelf. Gaze into it. What feelings are you experiencing? Does it make you feel happy or sad? What is in the picture? Does it remind you of a place you know? Or a person, someone you recognise? A friend, or family, or foe? This will come in useful when you start to do readings for other people because the card will tell you about the other person. You will be amazed at yourself.

Exercise

With a partner, choose a card. Look into the card, and begin to tell a story about it to your friend. Don't worry, if think you can't do it. Make it up! Write down as much as you can. Try not to stop writing even if you think they are silly things; keep writing; otherwise you stop the flow.

Remember, practice makes a man perfect.

Exercise

Now do a simple card reading

Before you use your cards, do the exercise to open up the chakras. Hold the cards in your hands for a moment or two until you start to feel the energies from the cards. Ask for the past reading energies to be removed so that you may do a fresh reading. Give the cards to your friend, and ask her to shuffle them, and, when she is ready, to lay them on the table.

Pick up the cards and lay them out in the simple Celtic cross spread.

First card in the middle represents the querier, the person you are doing the reading for.

Second card across the first depicts the situation they are in.

Third card is placed above and states what is happening in their life today.

Fourth card is laid beneath the main two and is the influence of the last three years with regard to their life today.

Fifth card to the left of the main cards is events that happened in the recent past.

Sixth card to the right shows stepping into the future.

Seventh eighth ninth and the tenth cards, in that order, from the right of the 6th and from bottom to top.

Start to read the cards in order from one to ten. You may add extra cards if you want as you get better at it.

It may be helpful at this stage to write prompts on your cards, for example, the simple meanings on the cards that you can remove at a later date. Don't forget, however, what you have interpreted from each individual card. Now is the time for testing these theories. You can start off by doing simple readings for your friends. The point is that the Tarot is a tool; they are prompting you, but you are doing the reading. In the beginning, I used the cards as a secondary reading. The funny thing I noticed was that after I had given a reading from the psyche, the cards that came out represented the issues I had already spoken of. Keep practicing as often as you can. This is a great tool and can speed your development. Always respect your cards. I keep mine wrapped in black velvet, in a box that belonged to my sister, who passed to spirit in 1975. However, you could make a silk bag for them, or wrap them in velvet—whatever pleases you.

CHAPTER 8

Remote Viewing

Now this is a good one. When I first started practicing this, I had some great fun. It was such a new idea to me. If you get really good at this, it can be very helpful. In the beginning, I didn't trust myself. One of the problems I had was that if I tried something and it didn't work for me, I gave up and went on to something new. This slowed me down, and I began losing confidence in myself. But after going back to the same exercise and trying again, I found I was actually getting some things right. This encouraged me, and with perseverance, I found I became quite good at it. This was when the fun started. I used to ask my friend to put something different in her house car or garden. Then, I would try to look for it in my mind's eye. Both of us worked on this. Sometimes, we really surprised ourselves with the results. As with everything, some days it will work better than others. Also, a point to remember is that not every single thing will be absolutely correct. Don't forget, we have a mind that interferes with what we are getting sometimes. Nevertheless, remote viewing is a fact that exists.

No one truly knows how remote viewing works, but it is fact that it does.

I remember, once I met a very special person while doing a course at the Arthur Findlay College, in Stansted. The following Sunday after coming home, I was resting on my bed when suddenly I saw a huge flash of white light. In that instant, I saw my special friend standing in a church talking to someone. I knew it was a psychic experience but did not realise what had happened until later on that evening. My friend rang me and asked what I was doing standing in his church! It was the exact same time as I had had my vision. Who says we can't be in two places at same time?

Remote viewing can be described as a form of mind travelling. From Suffolk to Newcastle in a flash is quite an achievement, I thought.

There are many uses for remote viewing, such as locating missing persons, collecting information, even crime solving.

It is recorded that stringent tests were carried out during the early 1900s. Early researchers included Sir William Crookes—an outstanding physicist and early pioneer of spiritualism, 18321919.

Military intelligence began to use mind travelling in the 1970s.

Also, it is said that well-known remote viewers were contacted to help locate other terrorists that may be at work, after the 11 September 2001 attacks.

Just a few good reasons to develop this practice, and the good news is that with dedication anyone can do it.

Exercise

This can be practiced on your own. Set aside a time when you will not be disturbed. The object of the exercise is to observe clearly what is there.

You can practice this anywhere and under any circumstances. Vary the times and situations as often as you can. A nice place to do this would be a garden or a park.

Imagine you are looking in a mirror, watching yourself and all that you are doing. Do not use a real mirror. Have a look around you, and observe as much as possible. Look at the whole picture as if you are not actually part of it. Notice everything about yourself and your surroundings. There are probably things that you have overlooked in the past. Practice this for about five minutes to start with.

This is a very beneficial exercise as it draws one away from focusing too much on one's own body. It helps you to take a look at yourself, and to how you interrelate to different situations in your world, and also enables you to hold several views of this in your mind. This is one of your most powerful tools. By using the mirror method, one is training the mind to fully observe the accuracy of what one sees. Sometimes, it is too easy to add things that are not there, that one thinks should be there, thereby missing what is really there? If we can't see what is in front of us, what chance have we of seeing something miles away. So the first thing is to become an accurate observer.

Exercise

You can do this with a friend.

This time, keep your eyes closed. Imagine that you are going to visit your friend whether you walk, get a bus, or drive there. Do everything as you would normally do for a real visit. For example, walk out to your car, open the door and get in. Start the engine, and drive in your normal way and take your usual route. It is very important that you do everything step by step. Don't just imagine yourself there. When you reach your friend's house, park your car, and walk towards your friend's garden. Look around the garden, notice everything in it. Smell and touch any flowers there may be. Have a good look around; your friend would have put something specific in an obvious place for you to see. What is it? You can stay as long as you like looking around. But don't forget that when it is time go home, you must return in exactly the same way as you came, step by step. Write down what you have noticed in the home, or garden, and compare notes the following day. Or if you like, taperecord your journey as you go along. Don't give up if you do not see anything at first. Just keep trying. Practice every day for a week, and see what happens. You may be surprised at your results. With determination, everyone can do remote viewing. It is a proven fact! So what are you waiting for?

CHAPTER 9

Inspirational Writing and Drawing

Even though I had developed my psychic ability to a high standard, like most people, I still had to work to earn a living. I worked as a live-in caretaker for a couple of years. It was while I was working at a respectable lady's residence that I began to suddenly write poetry. In my spare time, I used her library to rest in. The shelves were lined with books of famous actresses that Enid had met in her career as a theatre manager. There were all sorts of books and of a most interesting variety. Have you ever wished you could be thousands of miles away from a situation, but it seemed like there was no escape? Well, it was very peaceful here, like a much-needed haven to draw me away from reality. Enid was very independent as long as I satisfactorily saw to her needs; she was a very unobtrusive employer. I, therefore, found I had long hours to spend with nothing to do. My writing just seemed to flow out of the pen with hardly any thought. I found I was waking up in the morning with half a poem in my head. I began taking a pen and paper to bed with me and I woke up in the night to write down poems. Then the philosophy came like messages from above, which really helped me cope with my colourful life. It seemed once I started on my journey of enlightenment, things came along just when I needed them. We are not abandoned, yet we may feel we are. I found my understanding of the true meaning of life became clearer, for as I was helping other people, so I was helping myself. I kept up my meditation every day and often received inspiring words to comfort myself and others.

Exercise

This exercise can be done in a group, or with a friend, or on your own.

One person reads from a book some verses of poems, hymns, or an inspirational piece of writing.

Then close your eyes, and start off as you would a meditation, asking your higher self for some words of wisdom. Then imagine you are in a beautiful sunken garden with a waterfall in the middle of a lake. Sit down by this lake, and wait for someone to come and join you. You feel at peace with yourself as you silently take in the beauty of your surroundings. You are joined by a being of light who sits down beside you. He has something of importance to say to you.

After a ten minute break, you say goodbye to your mentor, knowing you will meet again. You hear the waterfall and you feel yourself coming back to yourself. Gradually open your eyes, and quietly take your pen and record all that has happened to you. This is a bit like a meditation, but you are asking for something specific. Whenever you work psychically, ask for what you want to achieve. Be grateful for all you receive. If you have practiced all the exercises I have shown you, your development has already improved your latent gifts. It seems to take longer for some than others, depending how dedicated one is. To become a successful consultant, there are many things to take into consideration. Believe me, nothing is beyond you; time, effort and a sense of responsibility is all you need.

Be aware that you don't necessarily need to make a conscious effort for inspirational writing to come. What I would advise you to do is be prepared for anything! Always have on you, a pencil and paper, or a recording device like a mobile phone. That will do. As soon as you realise these thoughts are running through your head, record them. You will be amazed by how informative your thoughts are. All the answers and advice is inside of you. No one knows you better than yourself.

Exercise

Here is another very useful exercise that writers often use when they suffer, what they call 'writers block'. I have found it a very useful tool for receiving philosophy. It occupies your mind until one forgets his presence to make way for one's higher self to intervene. Let me explain how it works.

When you go to bed at night, leave a pencil and paper by your bed. As soon as you open your eyes, without allowing time to lie there and think, pick up your pencil, and write the first thing that comes into your head.

When I first tried this, I just sat wondering where to begin; there were so many silly words that just popped into my head, for no apparent reason.

I was missing the point completely.

Then, I began writing all these silly things down. It was difficult at first; my hand ached, and it all seemed just so stupid. But I persevered. I kept on going, and after a while, I realised that my thoughts were beginning to make sense. I began writing possible solutions to questions I had been putting out. How amazing is that? Wouldn't you like to be able to use this tool? Well, you can if you want to.

Here is an example of my first attempt at this.

Inspirational art is just as interesting, and this is an exercise anyone can do.

Exercise

One can work on one's own or in a group. This one, however, is probably more fun in a group.

For this, one you will need paper and some pastels. I always find coloured card is good but white does just as well. It's a matter of preference.

Take a few minutes to sit quietly, and focus on what you would like to achieve.

Then, pick up a pastel and hold it sideways so the whole of the pastel is used and not just the end. Now, just take your pastel to and fro across the paper. Do not overwork. You will know when you want to stop. Try not to look at what you are doing. When you are finished, take a good look at it. Find out if you can see anything that resembles a face in the drawing. Now take a pencil, and outline it to make the face clearer.

Be aware of any thoughts that come into your mind, and write these down too.

Swap pictures and thoughts. When you allow your higher thoughts to control what you do, there are no boundaries and your results will astound you. Practice this often to stay in tune with it.

Exercise

You will need pencil and paper or paint. Have them at hand, but be inspired to use when the time comes.

If you have any inspirational music to play, take a few moments to listen to this first. Then keep it going throughout the exercise.

When you feel ready, take your medium and begin to draw, or paint, or anything that just flows from the hand. Don't try to achieve anything specific. You may not know what it is until you are almost finished. It may be a pattern, or a map, or a face, or an animal.

Do not have any preconceived ideas about what you are going to do.

Experiment with different music in different places, at home, or in the country, or town.

Practice in as many ways as you can to give this one a fair trial.

All these exercises are designed for you to try a few times to see how you get on with them. If you want to move on to the next one, that is fine. You may find you want to try them another time. Just keep practising and learning. Nothing is wasted. What you don't use now, you will probably find helpful later on somewhere in you progression.

CHAPTER 10

Consultations

So now, if you've come this far and kept up with your studies, you are able to give psychic readings. It maybe, however, that you don't want to, after all. Your time has not been wasted. You will have proved to yourself that you are psychic!

You have opened that door that said you may be able to do. Now that you have achieved this, you will know that virtually anything is possible if you believe in yourself. See yourself as successful in whatever you do.

Help yourself—be clear of what you want, and make positive moves to achieve this.

Use affirmations

Meditation

Do everything in the name of love.

Change your thoughts, and visualise what you want.

On the other hand, you may be raring to go ahead with your consultations. If so, then plough ahead. There's no stopping you now.

I have found it very important to keep up with my daily meditation. I speak to my guides every day to make sure I was attracting people who would benefit from my help. I needed to know that I was doing the right thing.

When I first started to do readings, I did them for everyone who asked. But they wanted a reading virtually every time they saw me, and while practice makes perfect, a psychic who doesn't know when to stop is like a dripping tap—no good to anyone. My energies soon became depleted, and I was beginning to think it wasn't worth it after all. A friend, who is also a medium, told me to start using my talent professionally, and that meant charging for my time. Well, she was right, of course. They steered clear when I mentioned money. But what I did find was that the people who really needed my help, came to me.

The first thing I did was to decorate the spare bedroom. I put in a desk, two comfortable chairs, and a small table. I did my daily meditation, healing, and readings here. I made proper appointments for people. The energies gradually built up in this room and had a lovely calming effect on people. On my desk, I had leaflets of all sorts of self-help groups. Everything about my work improved immensely. It proved to me that if I wanted people to take me seriously, I had to respect my gift and use it wisely.

I have been taught that it is a safe practice to have a table between you and your client when you do private readings. This is especially important if you work from home. Having said this, I have also found that if you respect your client and work in the name of love, one is usually protected. I believe like attracts like. People are coming to you for help and have usually been recommended by a friend.

It's always good to keep up to date with what's going on in this line of business. I attend other people's workshops and lectures and regularly go for courses at the Arthur Findlay College at Stansted. One is never finished learning and sharing experiences with old and new friends. This is, by far, the best way I have found of keeping ahead of things.

A few do's and don'ts for a responsible psychic.

Never tell a client they are going to have an accident.

Never tell a client someone close to them is going to die. One could find themselves in a great deal of trouble. Try to keep readings positive.

Negative messages will play on a client's mind. One could do more harm than good.

All clients should leave feeling positive and uplifted after a consultation. If the opposite is happening, you should seriously look at your own life to see what is going wrong. Maybe some more time should be dedicated to self-development through meditation and pure thoughts.

If you have kept up with your studies, then you have attained spiritual growth. You have learned so much and yet only just scratched the surface. As a medium and a channel for the spirit world, there is so much more to learn which is just as mind-blowing as the psychic phenomena. You will find that the most helpful teachers, apart from your own guides of course, are your clients.

The exercises I have shown in this book are only a few to get you started. One should take every opportunity to progress as we never finish learning. This is just the beginning of a fascinating new journey to the next stage of enlightenment.

FAQS

I am always asked lots of questions. Here are a few that may be helpful. If you have any queries that are not answered you can get in touch with me through my agent.

Q. Do you have to have a special gift to be psychic?

A. I believe everyone is psychic. In some, it is deeply buried and, therefore, may be more difficult to develop. But it is not impossible.

Q. What's the difference in being Psychic or telepathic.

A. First of all I would like to say that it is also a psychic ability.

There are many facets to psychic and this is one of them. Telepathy is an ability to use your mind and the mind of the person you are working with. So you pick things from their mind.

Being Psychic is being able to read from a person's inner self and using your own psyche to do this. (e.g., reading the aura, reading a person's personal things jewellery etc.) This is psychometry. There, first of all I would like to say that it is also a psychic ability.

There are so many ways of using ones psychic abilities. Everyone is Psychic to a certain extent and with the proper training one can enhance all sides of this.

Being a medium is however, totally different and this should not be confused with ones psychic ability.

Q. *How do you know its spirit talking to you and not imagination?*

A. Good question! Let me say first of all that mediumship could not work without your imagination. This is where spirit are able to put images words etc. The less imagination you have the harder to get through to you.

With practice you will also learn to experience the difference between the energies of Psychic and spirit. It is a knowing, a sensing, with practice you will get to know the difference. When a fully fledged medium is working they should be able to give exact evidence. Things no—one else knows about. Even if the recipient has to go and ask family etc., to check out the information when it is proved right what better evidence could there be. No one could pick that from one's mind!

Q. *What's the difference in being Psychic or telepathic.*

A. There are many facets to psychic and this is one of them. Telepathy is an ability to use your mind and the mind of the person you are working with. So you pick things from their mind.

Being Psychic is being able to read from a person's inner self and using your own psyche to do this. (e.g., reading the aura, reading a person's personal things jewellery etc.) This is psychometry. There are so many ways of using ones psychic abilities. Everyone is Psychic to a certain extent and with the proper training one can enhance all sides of this.

Being a medium is however, totally different and this should not be confused with ones psychic ability.

Q. *What is meant by an old soul?*

A. People who talk about an old soul usually mean an evolved spirit who has returned to earth many times. It is quicker to evolve through hardships experienced on the earth than to stay at or in the spirit world' and learn, but it is not essential. Each time one overcomes a great difficulty, one becomes more evolved. the more evolved the older the soul.

Q.   *How many guides do we have and how long do they stay with us?*

A.   Guides and helpers come to us for different reasons. We have one main guide who is with us for all time. It is someone we have had a strong connection with on all our soul journey.

Lots of helpers come along at various times depending on our interests. Like attracts like. If you study art you attract artists from the spirit world. When you become aware of this you may ask them for inspiration to influence you. They stay for as long as you need them. As your interests waver so do they. They go away and come back at a later date as you both evolve.

Q.   *What is the difference between guides and angels?*

A.   It is my understanding that guides are beings who have evolved more than we have so are able to teach us. We all evolve at various rates depending on our experiences. And we have to be taught at that level. It would be useless having a highly evolved spirit trying to influence us when are say a new spirit. For example, we have different teachers with different knowledge to teach our children. An expert in carpentry would probably be able to teach all ages of children but would adjust their communication skills otherwise the teaching would go right over their heads. In other words unable to reach them.

Angels are beings who have never incarnated, whose main work is protection. They are androgynous, having no specific gender. It is said that we all have our own Guardian Angel which we have from birth.

One should always satisfy themselves with their own teachings from within. If something does not sit comfortably with you just put it to one side for now.

These are just a few questions I have been asked but I am always happy to answer your questions through my agent or my website.

Lightning Source UK Ltd.
Milton Keynes UK
UKOW031555070612

193962UK00001B/171/P